DO
NOT
RISE

PITT POETRY SERIES

Ed Ochester, Editor

DO NOT RISE

BETH BACHMANN

UNIVERSITY OF PITTSBURGH PRESS

Published by the University of Pittsburgh Press, Pittsburgh, Pa., 15260
Manufactured in the United States of America
Printed on acid-free paper
10 9 8 7 6 5 4 3 2 1
ISBN 13: 978-0-8229-6328-8
ISBN 10: 0-8229-6328-0

to those
I lead my blood,

—PAUL CELAN,
    translated by
    Anne Carson

contents

i.

ii.

iii.

crisis

The air is hot and then it's cold.

The water wants out so open

your mouth and say, *snow.*

The water wants out right there

on the tongue. The flaw is always

breaking away. Watch the fire.

It wants out of the place

so it splinters like insects

out of a hole you pour light into.

Fragment, then drift or alarm.

revolution

The bite mark is unmistakable. Human and threatened. The clouds go
   on moving; thus, weather: anvil, horsetail, blood clot

above marsh, wood, field. A horse is useful. It gets the body to battle,
   but what the body does once

it gets there cannot be read by pattern. Some clouds are all energy we
   do not want everyone to possess. Little boy, keep your teeth

in your mouth. You are not my flesh and blood. Some flowers mimic a
   dead horse to imprison the blowfly. Take the flower first.

wild

Jar my mouth with your finger—petal

nest for the unborn bee after the mother is gone—darkly

burrow in what she laid

and sealed with mud—little bandage holding

the shape with blood—break it apart—one soldier locked to another:

one living, one dead. I said to the god,

I want you inside of me everywhere at once.

The god said, *I want all the power taken back*

and forth.
                    Your fingers are iron.
                                  I know.

open war

Open into apple blossom into   stigma,   bee, apple

into open mouth. Open war into calm above a water

unmanned. Another   failure on our part to commit

–cide by –cide b/y our own two hands. Open   as a body

after detonation, half of me   is   still here. The only

thing you have   to fear is yourself. Leave

the rest to me.

garden, and gun

You be the garden   I leave   my boots in when I walk   barefoot

after drought. *Do to me what no one has done.* What

can I do but undo   you by asking   for more

than was asked before?   Make the lake a cloud. The field needs rain

again. *Again?* Again. One   butterfly is torture,

flower-faced, a teaser. The wolf   cannot discern the dead

lavender from the living: neither is lavender. Red   is always
  hunger; yellow, possession,

but blue is nothing   if not   contrast. Only kill

what you can eat. How   do you know   what's poison? One
  skipper's tongue

is the length   of another's wingspan. Monarchs taste milky like the
  ditch they

feed in. *Glutton,*   never eat enough to kill, only sicken.

The wolf regards all movement as red   and beyond red, heat.

muse of arms

To swallow fire, first, listen to the direction of the wind.

If you are not careful, you can always hear the birds.

The trick is stillness. When I say, *wait, don't move,* don't

move. Pleasure is blinding but pain is a different beast.

At what point does the hand stop being the hand?

The crow's face in the bucket of wet coals is black

where petals do not cloak it. Where's the line? Fire-

walker, water, like blood, steadies heat. Fire-eater,

breathe in. First, place an ear to the tracks to count

the distance to the piston. The skin of a citrus cannot

conduct current. A broken circuit blocks the light.

shell

Fingers   in the mouth make mud

into a poultice to warm   the dead. Only water moving   fighter slow
   can't get out til

something goes in, above and below meeting at ice or lotus or   iris.
   Look at me

the way two soldiers paint one another's skin with wet hands until
   nothing is left

but the eyes. The dead we   burn; the living we bury in our faces.

shock

The cold-blooded butterfly has the eyes of a larger animal. It's so
easy to get

to ground blind, limb over limb.

Touching, with our guns over our shoulders, we are the body of
the trap—rifle,

antler, rifle. The buckeye

butterflies are back to back, drawing attention again to the body.
The fruit blushes

to attract a mouth, any mouth

that will finish it in dirt. *Honey oh orange honey sweetness*, the
eyes are all over

feasting. Fruit, old flower, quit acting like a girl.

oil

In the field of horseheads and empty drums,

neither was made of skin, so what

was the oil for? *My heart's welling,*

I said. *Give rope. Jackpump,*

then *consume me, love.* The thirsty birds

had no feathers

for wicking water. No feathers for camouflage or attraction

or flight. We hot-blued the gun

to protect it. Against the sky, the horseheads, the birds began to rust.

spill

heaven should have as much blood   beloved block after block we
   walk around

my neck a cut ruby a whole drop a   hundred years you said *the*
   ponies

were blue I said *under the skin* you said *under the sky*   last night
   I dreamt of swimming

first on my belly then on my back today was warmer   rain if he
   loved his body he loved

the body   pigmented in response block after block in the field no
   windows

no audience   involvement nothing abandoned to enter no iron bar
   beloved

by the body   chained *the mayfly nymphs have no mouth* I said you
   said *like an egg*

water

Let go fragmentation. I want the bomb   suit. I didn't
   know how much

it was capable of—the water   fracturing the rock, picking up
   the house and dropping it

in the middle of the bridge. There's no way   around it. Sensemaking is
   backwards

focused and in the armor, it's hard   to know where my body stops.
   Bottle after

bottle of the spring we swallowed, bag after bag   of bullets.
   All the flowers up

at the roots could live like this for awhile, if cold.

and war

I forgot about the water. It's all over   the map.

Belay me by knot, belay me by word,   belay me

across the river,   far anchor. Cross between

the animals' wide bones crossing   the river.

Nothing is so   beautiful. So much laughter, so much

ache to   fill with blood or food.   Water exposes

the force to   fire. Belay me   animal, belay me

heat,   belay me back of bitten swimmer.

sustainable

start here in each   other's mouth thirst

in place of speech before it   sometimes it stops there

the fickle birds dropping   what they just picked up cold

isn't it migration?   the wind what it failed to hold

back   what's this space

for if not mothering   desire? how long could it last

longer than a poem? silence *once*   *more not*

yet stop   *don't*

the tongue adhering to element before

after spring

dwelling

begins in delay. There's something

in my hand; hold it: fault I want

you to enter as the earth did the worm

whole and unstoppable til the beak bobbed

its body over and over—the peonies, in

heat, are disciplined as light in the fist and mouth

of the soldier. *Slow, slow.* The cover grows on me.

master, master

Nail me to the tree; I want to be forgiven. Sand?

I've seen   too much. Stranger, my scar is salt

water. I fear possession   so take me whole

for awhile. The right way is to use the rock

to block the body   from the bullet;

when I fire,   you fire. In close combat, it is now

or never. As in, *as a nation we are not now formally at war. Never
    look over*

an object when you can look around it. See that tree? Do not work
    against

the momentum of anything in motion. Two words: *try me.* Two words:
    Ask again. Nevermind.

Now; now. Kill

or be killed. The trees are burning   alive.

The soldier is both brute and champion.

ode

When we looked at the circle, we felt powerless. Earth or fist

our hands are bound together in protest. *Bare my throat*, I said,

in a face full of sand. I swallowed

too much water. The property   is private, the way we've come to

think of grief as nonviolence, absence,   lack,

fasting as an act

of attention. After awhile facedown in the field,

we roll over. All my favorite stars   are animals. I tire

of speech. Our bodies

are not on fire. We roll   onto the nest of the skylark

to hear it sing. When I said *you taste*

like a metal gate I meant   thank god there's a gate.

unspeakable

Two things that cannot be must be

first stone, then star. Mother of all monsters, father of all monsters, why

did you make me thus: tireless fox? Dog that eats whatever it wants,

unbeatable beast, at least we have the sky nightly, a view

of the whole battle. God cannot survive here.

He demands to be named. Unknown soldier, you hardly say you love
  me but you love me like the ice

the orchid takes slowly in its turning toward light.

In a garden, every bloom is somatic. I thought you wanted fire.

You want peace. You're facing a wall.

I am a species only you can claim.

humiliation

Where are the women in this war? The long limbs of the trees stripped
are the limbs of the trees. You can't have a war

without women. Where do you think all that blood comes from?
The trees in war are worse than the horses. You can kill a horse.

A horse can kill you. Most men have little use for metaphor.
Door go out. All fall down. Baby. Pray

nobody dare says the word. So many trees. The women are skinny
and there are more of you

than stars in the warfield, than shrapnel. Pigs?
I haven't seen pigs for months.

testimony

The flowers feel like sacrifice: opening and opening and
upending the golden light.

My mouth is also a cup. There's a buzzing on my tongue
where the honey should be.

Ask me anything. I'm yours for the hour. Or more,
like the flower. My skin's as thin

as a mussel shell; you can carve your face into
a valve. Try that on a petal.

The oils muffle the head.

bird,

build me a bower of toy soldiers, a song   of gunfire,

enough gray and green glass for a   shoreline. And inside,

a quiet breaking. Not a nest but a room   for what the water

gives and takes, breathing. All of it, metal   laden and halved,

clamped and cast, bones undressed in   plaster.

cleave

Stick or split? Ask the snow. The snow says, *blood   -shed*, but blood is
  not leaf or fur

or skin. The way the snow shows muscle is unnatural. It's not   like
  that. How else to know a thing? Look

what I can suffer with my hands. Mind   your conscience: it's one
  with parting one from another. Summer,

the tree pelts itself with apricots I skin   by the fistful til the
  bullet-ridden body is green again. My hand

is a magnet I couple to hotwire *filament anther light.* Stray   bullet
  jacketed in brass, could your mother pick

out your mouth hidden here on a higher limb? Would another   take
  you in, orphan apricot I can almost reach? Cut

a path in ice or water or cover or air   or meat. The sky I'm
  after is best viewed against.

sugar

Destroy it   so the body   can breathe.   I asked

for water   and you let go the wheel.   There's never

enough power to flood the field or drive   the blood into

its cage. It's impossible   to read the ruins without the missing

part— Bring the bones to be burned.   The flesh has too many
   holes.

Ruined,   we say, of the fruit   when it is all juice, of
   the body,

of the bed   sheets, of the word we cannot say   alone.

salt

The snow needs more
                     to oil

its throat into song. The birds
are gone
             and the deer are greedy,

eager to cauterize.
                 Slip me

a hinge. My hands are tied
like blackened flies. My fingers: hackle and feather.

Rock, rock, quiet water, rock. What rhymes
with rose

-flushed glass? The sun's a bloodbath.

why your room has a door

It's not the shore; it's the ocean   that opens. Devil, make a
    mountain

of me for the water to dwell   against. I became aware of my methods
    and the methods

changed me. Soldier, you make my body a map   on the floor.

It's what the door is for—   hesitation—a hand that wants

to be a mouth panting *pasture, food*, an ear

that dogs a woman. Water: hammer;   wrap your wrist. At
    parting, I insist

you call me by my first name.

landscape (hyperventilation)

You or I or the air says, *deeper*: breathe; the brain   needs blood.
  Mountain-sick, the moon

comes nearer, giving in. *More*   blood? Isn't it full? Where to put
  the mountain in relation to

the shadow, the human, the hunt, the hole in the fence?   Almanac
  says, if there is no death

in five days, there will be   *water. What for,* if not to smother or
  wash out a mouth

before it enters silent?   Moon, moon, keep moving   your fingers
  and they become a wheel

beneath the tiny legs of the stonefly. Moon opening, moon closing,
  nymph skin crawling over

the riverbed, you like to *say it*   first. In the mountains, it's easy to
  get caught   watching

something you shouldn't. It doesn't hurt the snow.

psyops

We can be so close to another body without

knowing it. Lush, we say of the field the color

of the dead, so green only the bindweed owns

it: strangle the light with black plastic or feed

the pigs pumpkin, the white flowers are slow

poison and chloroform's a sad love philter. The snow

is tired of fearing where to lie down. Bring me

a dog I can punish into a pleasing retriever.

The reader is not unlike the killer: you could be

anyone. Beauty is futile.

privacy

How much harm can entering
do? One cell, two,

and the whole law is broken in—
leg after leg,

the myrtle presses itself up from
the ground:

stampede. Horse, horse, horse, horse.
What are you turning

into? Inside me you murmur *so much
pain so much*

suffering. What makes the horses go
like that—fear

or fire? Circle me. What kills us is
not crush, but push.

interior design of temporary space (museum)

I love how sculpture makes you keep moving   around it—
    animal hip and shoulder and it

the stilled thing on the other side of the cage.   Be muse,
    be room, be opening, be space, not

to move around but through, as breath, as bodies'   erasure,
    words not to edge along, but hold in the hull.

Fire, I can taste when you've been feeding on wild   -flower.
    They're all over the boat. Tell me anything

you want. Shout it over the face of the animal. I want   to throw
    a stone through an old window. Watch me.

pony-shaped birdcage

Heartless horse no one   can break, I put my white and beating

songbird inside you. I put my hand,   open with seed. Now all of us

want more movement than the swing allows. I perch in your head and
   chirp, *stallion,*

but you will never go to war. I say, *the door is left open. You better run.*
   The bath is ticking

with hulls. You cannot rock me   tonight, to sleep.

public

Quiet: is it air or fire or one   feeding

the other? Unfold the paper: on one side,   pavilion;

on the other, wings. There's been a death.   You can tell

by the opening: speak. No shelter, only heat   swelling

in the ear. Parlor: confess;   between the butterfly

and the two-way mirror, it's brutal, the body's scar.   The sky

is not reflection though the bird flies into it like a rival.

bright one

Follow the belt. The bull's bloodshot eye is back. So much

is timing, the stars where they are

in winter: sailor, soldier, degrees

we chart. No desire for story, no explanation. The hunter

seen or unseen, either way, the bodies are struck

in this or that pattern. Hot stones, the horns and hooves where

we feel them.

restriction

If peony means binding, it's shameful

not to witness the wind mill through them til

we're short of breath. For a thing so submissive,

they have a way of holding our attention

by offering no closure: year after year

we cannot smother.

Black, in nature, no overtones, comes only at death

and after, the peonies remind us, big and satisfied.

dominance

Moon: horseshoe I hammer so we can ride.

Get your own muse. This one's desires require

nails. Moon, you are too cold face down

in the lake. How live is my anvil? It rings.

It rings. What makes a natural mover

is asymmetry. The balance of the winter will be warm.

iii.

gilt leather

Your skin smells skinned. Praise be the beast that gave its body
for your belt.

Praise be the heat that presses brass into gold
brand.

My scar is an army raised. It's okay to do what we do
to animals.

Little is forbidden. The tongue laps and laps
before lapsing

into speech. I do not want you
to dislike me.

The rain cannot desist. It touches like it never
had hands before.

hostage

Give me the baby. *Give me the gun.* He needs his singing

to sleep. It's endless, this one body on top of another. So much

of the war is waiting. The sky

in its habit of standing to, the light in its habit of refusal

when you beg it not to break.

Take away my son, Jesus, you would not understand,

I could kill a man. My love is inhuman; the water

is childlike, all that mud.

copperhead

Struck properly, the windpipe is copper

tubing.   I woke wanting a fitting all over

my green eyes, pennies   on my eyes,   but summer was long

October;   the snake had plenty

of places   to hide uncorroded and   not yet

slowed by cold. The second I say,   *put your hands on the back of
your head,*

look at me   not the weapon. Force me to open

my hand.   *We've been in love for some time now, remember?*

What, did you say, 'surrender'?

Do not rise.

ante-

God was right. We don't need any more

knowledge. The thing about the war is

you're not alone. Your bed is my bed

is another man's bed. The dead are lined up. Tomorrow's

work. Everyone's hungry. What can't be buried can be burned.

What can't be burned can be buried. God before and god after

we bathed in the same water, you who knows all my secrets,

who killed who and *where* and *why*, I said, god,

we're all hungry. You've got to eat.

afterlife

The honeysuckle is traceless
on the face of the deer. The scavenger's

head is unfeathered. I've cleared
a space. Flood it. The only blue offered

is burial. *We seldom see things.*
How are we to know they are there?

Eat, eat. Let me speak. I'll whisper

what I want to become.

wrap the throat

in black rubber; I have something to say over the noise of the engine,
I'm going in.

Heaven I cannot fathom—air measured like water, deep enough to
hide fire?

Power is always bound. Bayonet in the muzzle of the gun, you and me
are getting closer,

hand to hand, against. Wrap the neck in leather; the head is above
water. The head is moving

side to side, scanning the sky for enemy craft; wrap, then, the pilot's
throat in regulation silk.

The mic does not violate the mask.

hydra

of the war we said   the water

has many heads destroy one and two   more ripen thirsty flowers

winter is not a threat   here in this heat it takes so long for the head

and body to rise in constellation it's daylight the silver-white bird's gone

black   most things in nature have no meaning

still we wondered *how,*   *if*   *the answer*

was fear or love, to kill?

the cup always an offer prisoner   still

water is like leaves   a sound trap

alternative uses for ascot

Tie my wrists above the overturned canoe, for I am prone
to drowning
        and though I dress too lightly for the weather,

the hole in my pocket will not permit release.

Cradle wet rocks to ring the fire: startle me with gunshot.
No red-feathered bird can pressure this artery.

(army) trumpeter (flower)

To enter the garden, enclose it. The soldier is inside   me. A hundred
   hummingbird drones touched

to nectar, the red and orange flowers are murder   to remove.
   Mother, I hope you are warm.

Get some sleep, curious boy. My body   rests but the
   weapon's at ready. When the gap in the fence goes dark,

there's a head behind it. Soldier,   this is not my first war. Winter is
   as much a garden. In your white snow-suit, if I don't

know what I'm looking at, it's   working. *They're everywhere.*
They're murder.

If death could be one thing over and over, *this* and *this.*

clean

Thus, godly. Finally, no birds, no birdsong, no

snow. *Mine fire!* thus bite down

on the mask—rubber, bitter, metal, salt. Hot

to the touch, yet   keep it between the teeth. Mine

the mouth. Mine the palm-hollow. For once, escape,

not entry. Everyday air. No snow on the road, only falling.

coal

What else is there to offer, god, but the body

and everything in it? What's mine's

for mining. The wooden cages do not warn one another

of danger. *I'm burning* means *I'm burning*

not *beware*. The horses, though, in the field wear armor. The armor:

blood. What's that noise? Something announcing itself so

the beast won't startle. Keep your hand on the body

as you move around it. *Mother,*

the soldier says, *stand back.*

daffodil

bulb in the gut butt of the gun I am   numb soldier suicide is

everywhere   the narcissus   is narcotic *mother I am*   *writing*
   on the

veranda with no coat on not a cloud in the sky   all   day   I
   waited I waited

no box *carriage trap bus van cart motor etc. etc.* no   box
   yellow

flower in love with its own   ~~glowing~~ head

meal

Who belongs to this dead? Its leg

is confused with another leg. Toss it

in the pile for sorting. Something's missing.

Don't let the dog walk off with my bones. Who

put out the red bowl of water? I need that

fire. The wood for gripping. The twisting

bandages. Barber, there are rabbits in my tulips.

Hand me a bag of human hair. Keep the teeth.

In this heat, too much blood burns.

ode

Finish it. The blood is everywhere. Wild roses the hunter lets live.

Nurture or nature? Where'd you get that scar? The thing's willing

to die but something won't let it. It keeps slowly bleating out of the
  corner

of my eye. *Do not move my handkerchief. Do not make my dog bark.*

Noiseless wind. Gold leaf that foils the skin some animal's

gilding. Quietly, softly, do not make my shadow move, moon. Tell me

I'm not wrong. The ground doesn't know how to freeze.

welcome home (demobilization)

The yard is a wasteland. Abandon the white hydrangea

to its thirst. *Bleach* and *black*

have the same root

in *shine, flash, burn*. Meet

your son. He's fighting

sleep. Peace, too,

is an absence. Give me back

my war.

last, the mind is riderless. What is the forest for   if   not

a preserve in which to hunt   game? A horse in the forum is illegal:
   in the forest, lawless. *Always,*

you said,   lay and wait.   *Away,* I said, all the way over

or through   the field. Outside,   I am out of doors. Put the horse
   down.

It can no longer carry   weight. A little longer and it would've been
   morning.

energy

Sometimes, after snow, you find yourself in a field

of laughing gulls shaken and spat in a mass kill

and your boots are the only noise. It's like a bad joke

I cannot resist telling. Enough. Hunger is plenty.

Everything is dangerous. New moon, the red fox

is out walking. Extinction is nothing to the sea

other than exhaustion. Sometimes, it's a sand dune,

but even after storm, water's never silent. Rest

easy. Those sounds can't be human.

notes

"to those / I lead my blood" is Anne Carson's translation of Paul Celan's "Alle die Schlafgestalten, kristallin," ("All Those Sleep Shapes, Crystalline"), which appears in Carson's *Economy of the Unlost* (Princeton: Princeton University Press, 1999), used with permission.

"and war" and "shell" were written in response to *U.S. Army Field Manual* chapters on "Mountain Stream Crossings" and "Cover, Concealment and Camouflage." The first line of "copperhead" is a paraphrase of the field manual *Kill or Get Killed*, which also informs "master, master."

"shock": "As late as the nineteenth century, orange vendors in Palermo, Sicily, advertised their wares with the strange cry, 'Here's the honey!' which was very similar to the cry of the orange vendors in Cairo, who yelled 'Honey! Oh, oranges! Honey!'" (Pierre Laszlo, *Citrus: A History* [Chicago: University of Chicago Press, 2007]).

"cleave": "Grant us the power to prove, by poison gases, / The needlessness of *shedding* human blood" (Siegfried Sassoon, "Asking For It," 1934).

The "pony-shaped birdcage" is attributed to Frederic Weinberg, circa 1950.

"copperhead": "Stay, O sweet, and do not rise!" (John Donne, "Daybreak"). Also, "Stand down. Stand by me." (Cassius Clay singing "Stand by Me," 1964).

The italicized lines in "afterlife" are taken from "How to Know the Wild Things" from *The Woodcraft Manual for Boys* by Ernest Thompson Seton, 1917.

"hydra": "A poem need not have a meaning and like most things in nature often does not have" (Wallace Stevens, "Adagia," 1955).

The italicized lines in "daffodil" are from Wilfred Owen's letter to his mother dated December 24, 1909. The line, "Mother, I hope you are warm," in "(army) trumpeter (flower)" is taken from Owen's final letter home. The last words of "coal" come from Wilfred Owen's letter to his mother dated June 24, 1918.

The italicized lines in "ode" (ii) are taken from *The Book of Songs*, Ode 23, translated from the Chinese by James Legge, 1861.

acknowledgments

Grateful acknowledgement to Ed Ochester and to the editors
where these poems first appeared:

> *American Poetry Review*: "cleave" and "interior design
> of temporary space (museum)"; *Blackbird*: "bright one,"
> "restriction," and "afterlife"; *The Book of Scented Things*
> (eds. Jehanne Dubrow and Lindsay Lusby): "unspeakable";
> *Boston Review*: "spill"; *Crazyhorse*: "testimony," "gilt
> leather," "oil," and "copperhead"; *Missouri Review*:
> "alternative uses for ascot"; *Paris-American*: "sugar," "salt,"
> and "landscape (hyperventilation)"; *Ploughshares*: "why
> your room has a door," "ode" (i), and "energy"; *Southern
> Review*: "sustainable," "clean," and "meal"; *TriQuarterly*:
> "shell" and "coal."

"why your room has a door" was also reprinted as a limited
edition broadside by the Rose O'Neill Literary House in
commemoration of AWP Boston 2013.

Do Not Rise received the 2011 Alice Fay Di Castagnola Award
from the Poetry Society of America, and the poem "muse of
arms" appeared on their website.

"water," "and war," "hostage," "ante-," "bird," "(army) trumpeter
(flower)," "shock," "daffodil," "public," "dominance," and "master,
master" first appeared in *Flaw*, a limited-edition chapbook
released by Organic Weapon Arts, edited by Jamaal May and
Tarfia Faizullah, 2014.

Many, many thanks to everyone at Pitt, Vanderbilt, Sewanee, and Bread Loaf and to those who read along the way and kept me going: Robert Hass, Carl Phillips, Elizabeth Willis, Jehanne Dubrow, Tom Johnston, and Nick Flynn. And to Brian. Peace is next.